Machine Learning

Guide for Beginners with R/Python/Scala

Contents

Chapter 1: Machine Learning 5

  1.1   What is Machine Learning? 6

    1.1.1   History of Machine Learning 7

    1.1.2   ELIZA 8

    1.1.3   Neural Networks......................................9

    1.1.4   Statistical AI 9

    1.1.5   Big Data 10

    1.1.6   Current Status 10

    1.1.7   Terminology..11

  1.2   Why use Machine Learning? 13

    1.2.1   Applications of Machine Learning 13

  1.3   Key Elements of Machine Learning 15

  1.4   Types of Learning 16

  1.5   Machine Learning in Practice 17

  1.6   What is inductive learning.................................18

Chapter 2: Mathematical Foundation for Machine Learning & AI..19

  2.1 Introduction 20

    2.1.1 Why Worry About the Maths? 20

    2.1.2 What Level of Maths Do You Need?................21

  2.2 Linear Algebra 23

    2.2.1 Notation 24

    2.2.2 Vector Space..25

    2.2.3 Euclidean Space...27

    2.2.4 Subspaces..27

    2.2.5 Matrices..28

    2.2.6 Vector 28

    2.2.7 Tensors 29

    2.2.8 Computational Rules 30

    2.2.9 Summary 33

  2.3 Multivariate Calculus...34

    2.3.1 Derivative 35

    2.3.2 Machine Learning use Cases 36

2.3.3 Chain Rule..37
2.3.4 Gradient 37
2.3.5 Partial Derivative 38
2.4 Probability Theory 38
2.4.1 Frequentist Probabilities 39
2.4.2 Conditional Probabilities 39
2.4.3 Dependent and Independent Events...............40
2.4.4 Distributions 40
2.4.5 Basic Rules & Models 41
Chapter 3: Programming Languages for Machine
Learning..43
3.1 Programming Language..44
3.2 Best Programming Languages for Machine
Learning..45
3.2.1 Python 45
3.2.2 R 46
3.2.3 Lisp 46
3.2.4 Java..47
3.2.5 Scala 47
3.3 Tools for Machine Learning..................................48
3.3.1 TensorFlow 48
3.3.2 Keras..49
3.3.3 SciKit-Learn..50
3.3.4 Edward 51
3.3.5 Lime 52
Chapter 4: Introduction to Python/R/Scala.....................53
4.1 Introduction to Python 54
4.1.1 Environment Setup..54
4.1.2 Writing First Program 54
4.2 Introduction to R 55
4.2.1 Environment Setup..55
4.2.2 Writing First Program 57
4.3 Scala 58
4.3.1 Environment Setup..58

4.3.2 Writing First Program 61
Chapter 5: Introduction to MLlib (Apache Spark) 63
5.1   Introduction...64
5.1.1   Features of Apache Spark.........................64
5.2   MLlib...66
5.2.1   Overview 66
5.2.2   Spark MLlib Tools 66
5.2.3   MLlib Algorithms 67
Chapter 6: Overview of Available ML Libraries 73
6.1 Libraries of Python 74
6.1.1 TensorFlow 74
6.1.2 Scikit-learn...75
6.1.3 Theano..75
6.1.4 Pylearn2...75
6.1.5 Pyevolve 76
6.1.6 NuPIC..77
6.1.7 Numpy 77
6.1.8 Eli5..78
6.1.9 PyTorch...78
6.1.10 Pandas 79
6.1.11 Pattern...79
6.1.12 Caffe 80
Chapter 7: Conclusion 81
7.1 Conclusion 82

Chapter 1: Machine Learning

1.1 What is Machine Learning?

Before we take a look at the details of various machine learning methods, let's start by looking at what machine learning is, and what it isn't. Machine learning is often categorized as a subfield of artificial intelligence, but I find that categorization can often be misleading at first brush. The study of machine learning certainly arose from research in this context, but in the data science application of machine learning methods, it's more helpful to think of machine learning as a means of building models of data. Fundamentally, machine learning involves building mathematical models to help understand data. "Learning" enters the fray when we give these models tunable parameters that can be adapted to observed data; in this way the program can be considered to be "learning" from the data. Once these models have been fit to previously seen data, they can be used to predict and understand aspects of newly observed data. I'll leave to the reader the more philosophical digression regarding the extent to which this type of mathematical, model-based "learning" is similar to the "learning" exhibited by the human brain.

Machine learning is an application of artificial intelligence (AI) that provides systems the ability to automatically learn and improve from experience without being explicitly programmed. Machine learning focuses on the development of computer programs that can access data and use it learn for themselves.

The process of learning begins with observations or data, such as examples, direct experience, or instruction, in order to look for patterns in data and make better decisions in the future based on the examples that we provide. The primary aim is to allow the computers learn automatically without human intervention or assistance and adjust actions accordingly.

1.1.1   History of Machine Learning

The history of the field of Machine Learning is a fascinating story. In 1946 the first computer system ENIAC was developed. At that time the word 'computer' meant a human being that performed numerical computations on paper and ENIAC was called a numerical computing machine. This machine was manually operated, i.e. a human would make connections between parts of the machine to perform computations. The idea at that time was that human thinking and learning could be rendered logically in such a machine.

In 1950 Alan Turing proposed a test to measure its performance. The Turing test is based on the idea that we can only determine if a machine can actually learn if we communicate with it and cannot distinguish it from another human. Although, there have not been any systems that passed the Turing test many interesting systems have been developed.

1.1.2   ELIZA

Around 1952 Arthur Samuel (IBM) wrote the first game-playing program, for checkers, to achieve sufficient skill to challenge a world champion. Samuel's machines learning programs worked remarkably well and were helpful in improving the performance of checkers players. Another milestone was the ELIZA system developed in the early 60's by Jospeph Weizenbaum. ELIZA simulated a psychotherapist by using tricks like string substitution and canned responses based on keywords. When the original ELIZA first appeared, some people actually mistook her for human.

The illusion of intelligence works best, however, if you limit your conversation to talking about yourself and your life. Although the overall performance of ELIZA was disappointing, it was a nice proof of concept. Later on, many other systems have been developed. Important was the work of the group of Ted Shortliffe on MYCIN (Stanford). They demonstrated the power of rule-based systems for knowledge representation and inference in the domain of medical diagnosis and therapy. This system is often called the first expert system.

1.1.3   Neural Networks

At the same time when the expert systems were developed, other approaches to Machine Learning emerged. In 1957 Frank Rosenblatt invented the Perceptron at the Cornell Aeronautical Laboratory. The Perceptron is a very simple linear classifier but it was shown that by combining a large number of them in a network a powerful model could be created.

Neural network research went through many years of stagnation after Marvin Minsky and his colleagues showed that neural networks could not solve problems such as the XOR problem. However, several modifications have been produced later on that solve XOR and many more difficult problems.

1.1.4   Statistical AI

In the early 90's Machine Learning became very popular again due to the intersection of Computer Science and Statistics. This synergy resulted in a new way of thinking in AI: the probabilistic approach. In this approach uncertainty in the parameters is incorporated in the models. The field shifted to a more data-driven approach as compared to the more knowledge-driven expert systems developed earlier. Many of the current success stories of Machine Learning are the result of the ideas developed at that time.

1.1.5   Big Data

Statistical AI is a center piece of Big Data analysis: as a result of the exponential growth in the amount of data that is available for scientific research, the sciences are on the brink of huge changes. That applies to all disciplines. In biology, for example, there will shortly be around 1 Exabyte of genomics data (10 to the power of 18 bytes) in the world. In 2024 the next generation of radio telescopes will produce in excess of 1 Exabyte per day. To deal with this data deluge, a new scientific discipline is taking shape. Big Data Science aims to develop new methods to store those substantial amounts, and to quickly find, analyze and validate complex patterns in Big Data.

1.1.6   Current Status

The study of Machine Learning has grown from the efforts of a handful of computer engineers exploring whether computers could learn to play games and mimic the human brain, and a field of statistics that largely ignored computational considerations, to a broad discipline that has produced fundamental statistical-computational theories of learning processes.

Many of the new learning algorithms, such as support vector machines and Bayesian networks, are routinely used in commercial systems. We envisage that in the upcoming years Machine

Learning will play a major role in the discovery of knowledge from the wealth of data that is currently available in a diverse amount of application areas.

1.1.7 Terminology

The following terms will come up repeatedly in our discussion of effective machine learning:

- **Instance:** The thing about which you want to make a prediction. For example, the instance might be a web page that you want to classify as either "about cats" or "not about cats".

- **Label:** An answer for a prediction task either the answer produced by a machine learning system, or the right answer supplied in training data. For example, the label for a web page might be "about cats".

- **Feature:** A property of an instance used in a prediction task. For example, a web page might have a feature "contains the word 'cat'".

- **Feature Column:** A set of related features, such as the set of all possible countries in which users might live. An example may have one or more features present in a feature column. "Feature column" is Google-specific terminology. A feature column is referred to as a "namespace" in

11

the VW system (at Yahoo/Microsoft), or a field.

- **Example:** An instance (with its features) and a label.
- **Model:** A statistical representation of a prediction task. You train a model on examples then use the model to make predictions.
- **Metric:** A number that you care about. May or may not be directly optimized.
- **Objective:** A metric that your algorithm is trying to optimize.
- **Pipeline:** The infrastructure surrounding a machine learning algorithm. Includes gathering the data from the front end, putting it into training data files, training one or more models, and exporting the models to production.
- **Click-through Rate:** The percentage of visitors to a web page who click a link in an ad.

1.2 Why use Machine Learning?

Machine learning is needed for tasks that are too complex for humans to code directly. Some tasks are so complex that it is impractical, if not impossible, for humans to work out all of the nuances and code for them explicitly. So instead, we provide a large amount of data to a machine learning algorithm and let the algorithm work it out by exploring that data and searching for a model that will achieve what the programmers have set it out to achieve.

How well the model performs is determined by a cost function provided by the programmer and the task of the algorithm is to find a model that minimizes the cost function.

1.2.1 Applications of Machine Learning

Machine learning is an application of artificial intelligence (AI) that provides systems the ability to automatically learn and improve from experience without being explicitly programmed. Machine learning focuses on the development of computer programs that can access data and use it learn for themselves.

The process of learning begins with observations or data, such as examples, direct experience, or instruction, in order to look for patterns in data and make better decisions in the future based on the examples that we provide. The primary aim is to allow the computers learn automatically without human intervention or assistance and adjust actions accordingly.

Sample applications of machine learning:

- **Web search:** ranking page based on what you are most likely to click on.
- **Computational biology:** rational design drugs in the computer based on past experiments.
- **Finance:** decide who to send what credit card offers to. Evaluation of risk on credit offers. How to decide where to invest money.
- **E-commerce:** Predicting customer churn. Whether or not a transaction is fraudulent.
- **Space exploration:** space probes and radio astronomy.
- **Robotics:** how to handle uncertainty in new environments. Autonomous. Self-driving car.
- **Information extraction:** Ask questions over databases across the web.
- **Social networks:** Data on relationships and preferences. Machine learning to extract value from data.
- **Debugging:** Use in computer science problems like debugging. Labor intensive process. Could suggest where the bug could be.

1.3 Key Elements of Machine Learning

There are tens of thousands of machine learning algorithms and hundreds of new algorithms are developed every year.

Every machine learning algorithm has three components:

- **Representation:** how to represent knowledge. Examples include decision trees, sets of rules, instances, graphical models, neural networks, support vector machines, model ensembles and others.
- **Evaluation:** the way to evaluate candidate programs (hypotheses). Examples include accuracy, prediction and recall, squared error, likelihood, posterior probability, cost, margin, entropy k-L divergence and others.
- **Optimization:** the way candidate programs are generated known as the search process. For example, combinatorial optimization, convex optimization, constrained optimization.
- All machine learning algorithms are combinations of these three components. A framework for understanding all algorithms.

1.4 Types of Learning

There are four types of machine learning:

- **Supervised learning:** (also called inductive learning) Training data includes desired outputs. This is spam this is not, learning is supervised.
- **Unsupervised learning:** Training data does not include desired outputs. Example is clustering. It is hard to tell what is good learning and what is not.
- **Semi-supervised learning:** Training data includes a few desired outputs.
- **Reinforcement learning:** Rewards from a sequence of actions. AI types like it, it is the most ambitious type of learning.
- **Supervised learning** is the most mature, the most studied and the type of learning used by most machine learning algorithms. Learning with supervision is much easier than learning without supervision.
- **Inductive Learning** is where we are given examples of a function in the form of data (x) and the output of the function (f(x)). The goal of inductive learning is to learn the function for new data (x).
- **Classification:** when the function being learned is discrete.
- **Regression:** when the function being learned is continuous.
- **Probability Estimation:** when the output of the function is a probability.

1.5 Machine Learning in Practice

Machine learning algorithms are only a very small part of using machine learning in practice as a data analyst or data scientist. In practice, the process often looks like:

- **Start Loop**
- ✓ Understand the domain, prior knowledge and goals. Talk to domain experts. Often the goals are very unclear. You often have more things to try then you can possibly implement.
- ✓ Data integration, selection, cleaning and pre-processing. This is often the most time-consuming part. It is important to have high quality data. The more data you have, the more it sucks because the data is dirty. Garbage in, garbage out.
- ✓ Learning models. The fun part. This part is very mature. The tools are general.
- ✓ Interpreting results. Sometimes it does not matter how the model works as long it delivers results. Other domains require that the model is understandable. You will be challenged by human experts.
- ✓ Consolidating and deploying discovered knowledge. The majority of projects that are successful in the lab are not used in practice. It is very hard to get something used.
- **End Loop**

It is not a one-shot process, it is a cycle. You need to run the loop until you get a result that you can use in practice. Also, the data can change, requiring a new loop.

1.6 What is inductive learning

From the perspective of inductive learning, we are given input samples (x) and output samples (f(x)) and the problem is to estimate the function (f). Specifically, the problem is to generalize from the samples and the mapping to be useful to estimate the output for new samples in the future.

In practice it is almost always too hard to estimate the function, so we are looking for very good approximations of the function.

Some practical examples of induction are:

- Credit risk assessment.
- ✓ The x is the properties of the customer.
- ✓ The f(x) is credit approved or not.
- Disease diagnosis.
- ✓ The x are the properties of the patient.
- ✓ The f(x) is the disease they suffer from.
- Face recognition.
- ✓ The x are bitmaps of people's faces.
- ✓ The f(x) is to assign a name to the face.
- Automatic steering.
- ✓ The x are bitmap images from a camera in front of the car.
- ✓ The f(x) is the degree the steering wheel should be turned.

Chapter 2: Mathematical Foundation for Machine Learning & AI

2.1 Introduction

The future for AI is extremely promising and it isn't far from when we have our own robotic companions. This has pushed a lot of developers to start writing codes and start developing for AI and ML programs. However, learning to write algorithms for AI and ML isn't easy and requires extensive programming and mathematical knowledge.

Mathematics plays an important role as it builds the foundation for programming for these two streams. And in this course, we've covered exactly that. We designed a complete course to help you master the mathematical foundation required for writing programs and algorithms for AI and ML.

The book covers three main mathematical theories: Linear Algebra, Multivariate Calculus and Probability Theory.

2.1.1 Why Worry About the Maths?

There are many reasons why the mathematics of Machine Learning is important and I will highlight some of them below:

- Selecting the right algorithm which includes considering accuracy, training time, model complexity, number of parameters and number of features.
- Choosing parameter settings and validation strategies.
- Identifying underfitting and overfitting by understanding the Bias-Variance tradeoff.
- Estimating the right confidence interval and uncertainty.

2.1.2 What Level of Maths Do You Need?

The main question when trying to understand an interdisciplinary field such as Machine Learning is the amount of maths necessary and the level of maths needed to understand these techniques. The answer to this question is multidimensional and depends on the level and interest of the individual. Research in mathematical formulations and theoretical advancement of Machine Learning is ongoing and some researchers are working on more advance techniques. I will state what I believe to be the minimum level of mathematics needed to be a Machine Learning Scientist/Engineer and the importance of each mathematical concept.

- **Linear Algebra:** In ML, Linear Algebra comes up everywhere. Topics such as Principal Component Analysis (PCA), Singular Value Decomposition (SVD), Eigen decomposition of a matrix, LU Decomposition, QR Decomposition/Factorization, Symmetric Matrices, Orthogonalization & Orthonormalization, Matrix Operations, Projections, Eigenvalues & Eigenvectors, Vector Spaces and Norms are needed for understanding the optimization methods used for machine learning. The amazing thing about Linear Algebra is that there are so many online resources.

- **Probability Theory and Statistics:** Machine Learning and Statistics aren't very different fields.

Actually, someone recently defined Machine Learning as 'doing statistics on a Mac'. Some of the fundamental Statistical and Probability Theory needed for ML are Combinatorics, Probability Rules & Axioms, Bayes' Theorem, Random Variables, Variance and Expectation, Conditional and Joint Distributions, Standard Distributions (Bernoulli, Binomial, Multinomial, Uniform and Gaussian), Moment Generating Functions, Maximum Likelihood Estimation (MLE), Prior and Posterior, Maximum a Posteriori Estimation (MAP) and Sampling Methods.

- **Multivariate Calculus:** Some of the necessary topics include Differential and Integral Calculus, Partial Derivatives, Vector-Values Functions, Directional Gradient, Hessian, Jacobian, Laplacian and Lagragian Distribution.

- **Algorithms and Complex Optimizations:** This is important for understanding the computational efficiency and scalability of our Machine Learning Algorithm and for exploiting sparsity in our datasets. Knowledge of data structures (Binary Trees, Hashing, Heap, Stack etc.), Dynamic Programming, Randomized & Sublinear Algorithm, Graphs, Gradient/Stochastic Descents and Primal-Dual methods are needed.

- **Others:** This comprises of other Math topics not covered in the four major areas described above. They include Real and Complex Analysis (Sets and Sequences, Topology, Metric Spaces, Single-

Valued and Continuous Functions, Limits, Cauchy Kernel, Fourier Transforms), Information Theory (Entropy, Information Gain), Function Spaces and Manifolds.

2.2 Linear Algebra

In this section we present important classes of spaces in which our data will live and our operations will take place: vector spaces, metric spaces, normed spaces, and inner product spaces. Generally speaking, these are defined in such a way as to capture one or more important properties of Euclidean space but in a more general way. Linear Algebra is a continuous form of mathematics and is applied throughout science and engineering because it allows you to model natural phenomena and to compute them efficiently. Because it is a form of continuous and not discrete mathematics, a lot of computer scientists don't have a lot of experience with it. Linear Algebra is also central to almost all areas of mathematics like geometry and functional analysis. Its concepts are a crucial prerequisite for understanding the theory behind Machine Learning, especially if you are working with Deep Learning Algorithms. You don't need to understand Linear Algebra before getting started with Machine Learning, but at some point, you may want to gain a better understanding of how the different Machine Learning algorithms really work under the hood. This will help you to make better decisions during a Machine Learning system's development. So, if you really want to be a professional in this field, you will have to master the parts of Linear Algebra that are important for Machine Learning. In Linear Algebra, data is represented by linear equations, which are presented in the form of matrices and vectors.

2.2.1 Notation

Notation	Meaning
R	set of real numbers
R_n	set (vector space) of n-tuples of real numbers, endowed with the usual inner product
$R_{m \times n}$	set (vector space) of m-by-n matrices
δ_{ij}	Kronecker delta, i.e. $\delta_{ij} = 1$ if $i = j$, 0 otherwise
$\nabla f(\mathbf{x})$	gradient of the function f at $\mathbf{x}$
$\nabla^2 f(\mathbf{x})$	Hessian of the function f at $\mathbf{x}$
$\mathbf{A}_>$	transpose of the matrix $\mathbf{A}$
Ω	sample space
$P(A)$	probability of event A
$p(X)$	distribution of random variable X
$p(x)$	probability density/mass function evaluated at x
A_c	complement of event A
$A \cup' B$	union of A and B, with the extra requirement that $A \cap B = \emptyset$
$E[X]$	expected value of random variable X
$Var(X)$	variance of random variable X
$Cov(X, Y)$	covariance of random variables X and Y

2.2.2 Vector Space

Vector spaces are the basic setting in which linear algebra happens. A vector space V is a set (the elements of which are called **vectors**) on which two operations are defined: vectors can be added together, and vectors can be multiplied by real numbers[1] called **scalars**. V must satisfy

(i) There exists an additive identity (written **0**) in V such that $\mathbf{x} + \mathbf{0} = \mathbf{x}$ for all $\mathbf{x} \in V$

(ii) For each $\mathbf{x} \in V$, there exists an additive inverse (written $-\mathbf{x}$) such that $\mathbf{x} + (-\mathbf{x}) = \mathbf{0}$

(iii) There exists a multiplicative identity (written 1) in R such that $1\mathbf{x} = \mathbf{x}$ for all $\mathbf{x} \in V$

(iv) Commutativity: $\mathbf{x} + \mathbf{y} = \mathbf{y} + \mathbf{x}$ for all $\mathbf{x}, \mathbf{y} \in V$

(v) Associativity: $(\mathbf{x} + \mathbf{y}) + \mathbf{z} = \mathbf{x} + (\mathbf{y} + \mathbf{z})$ and $\alpha(\beta\mathbf{x}) = (\alpha\beta)\mathbf{x}$ for all $\mathbf{x}, \mathbf{y}, \mathbf{z} \in V$ and $\alpha, \beta \in$ R

(vi) Distributivity: $\alpha(\mathbf{x} + \mathbf{y}) = \alpha\mathbf{x} + \alpha\mathbf{y}$ and $(\alpha + \beta)\mathbf{x} = \alpha\mathbf{x} + \beta\mathbf{x}$ for all $\mathbf{x}, \mathbf{y} \in V$ and $\alpha, \beta \in$ R

A set of vectors $\mathbf{v}_1, ..., \mathbf{v}_n \in V$ is said to be **linearly independent** if

$$\alpha_1 \mathbf{v}_1 + \cdots + \alpha_n \mathbf{v}_n = \mathbf{0} \qquad \text{implies} \qquad \alpha_1 = \cdots = \alpha_n = 0.$$

---

[1] More generally, vector spaces can be defined over any **field** F. We take F = R in this document to avoid an unnecessary diversion into abstract algebra.

The **span** of $v_1,...,v_n \in V$ is the set of all vectors that can be expressed of a linear combination of them:

$$\text{span}\{v_1,...,v_n\} = \{v \in V : \exists \alpha_1,...,\alpha_n$$
$$\text{such that } \alpha_1 v_1 + \cdots + \alpha_n v_n = v\}$$

If a set of vectors is linearly independent and its span is the whole of V, those vectors are said to be a **basis** for V. In fact, every linearly independent set of vectors forms a basis for its span.

If a vector space is spanned by a finite number of vectors, it is said to be **finite-dimensional**. Otherwise it is **infinite-dimensional**. The number of vectors in a basis for a finite-dimensional vector space V is called the **dimension** of V and denoted $\dim V$.

$$[2 \quad 5] \text{ -> Row Vector}$$

$$\begin{bmatrix} 1 & -8 \\ 7 & 3 \end{bmatrix} \text{ -> Matrix (No. of rows x No. of Columns)}$$

$$\begin{matrix} 1 & 0 & 0 \\ 0 & 1 & 0 \\ 0 & 0 & 1 \end{matrix}$$

2.2.3 Euclidean Space

Euclidean space is used to mathematically represent physical space, with notions such as distance, length, and angles. Although it becomes hard to visualize for $n > 3$, these concepts generalize mathematically in obvious ways. Even when you're working in more general settings than R^n, it is often useful to visualize vector addition and scalar multiplication in terms of 2D vectors in the plane or 3D vectors in space.

2.2.4 Subspaces

Vector spaces can contain other vector spaces. If V is a vector space, then $S \subseteq V$ is said to be a **subspace** of V if

   (i) $\mathbf{0} \in S$

   (ii) S is closed under addition: $\mathbf{x}, \mathbf{y} \in S$ implies $\mathbf{x} + \mathbf{y} \in S$

   (iii) S is closed under scalar multiplication: $\mathbf{x} \in S, \alpha \in R$ implies $\alpha\mathbf{x} \in S$

Note that V is always a subspace of V, as is the trivial vector space which contains only $\mathbf{0}$.

As a concrete example, a line passing through the origin is a subspace of Euclidean space.

If U and W are subspaces of V, then their sum is defined as

$$U + W = \{\mathbf{u} + \mathbf{w} \mid \mathbf{u} \in U, \mathbf{w} \in W\}$$

2.2.5 Matrices

Matrices play a central role in linear algebra. They can be used to compactly represent systems of linear equations. Before we discuss some of these interesting topics, let us first define what a matrix is and what kind of operations we can do with matrices.

A Matrix is an ordered 2D array of numbers and it has two indices. The first one points to the row and the second one to the column. For example, M23 refers to the value in the second row and the third column, which is 8 in the yellow graphic above. A Matrix can have multiple numbers of rows and columns. Note that a Vector is also a Matrix, but with only one row or one column.

The Matrix in the example in the yellow graphic is also a 2- by 3-dimensional Matrix (rows x columns). Below you can see another example of a Matrix along with its notation:

$$\begin{bmatrix} u11 & \cdots & u1n \\ \vdots & \ddots & \vdots \\ um1 & \cdots & umn \end{bmatrix}$$

2.2.6 Vector

A Vector is an ordered array of numbers and can be in a row or a column. A Vector has just a single index, which can point to a specific value within the Vector. For example, V2 refers to the second value within the Vector, which is -8 in the graphic above

$$\begin{bmatrix} x1 \\ \vdots \\ xn \end{bmatrix}$$

2.2.7 Tensors

You can think of a Tensor as an array of numbers, arranged on a regular grid, with a variable number of axes. A Tensor has three indices, where the first one points to the row, the second to the column and the third one to the axis. For example, T232 points to the second row, the third column, and the second axis

3	1	4	1
5	9	2	6
4	7	6	3
1	4	8	9
7	2	3	2
7	2	3	0

tensor of dimensions [6,4]

Tensor is the most general term for all of these concepts above because a Tensor is a multidimensional array and it can be a Vector and a Matrix, depending on the number of indices it has. For example, a first-order Tensor would be a Vector (1 index). A second-order Tensor is a Matrix (2 indices) and third-order Tensors (3 indices) and higher are called Higher-Order Tensors (3 or more indices).

2.2.8 Computational Rules

2.2.8.1 Matrix Scalar Operations

Multiplying a Matrix by a Vector can be thought of as multiplying each row of the Matrix by the column of the Vector. The output will be a Vector that has the same number of rows as the Matrix.

2.2.8.2 Matrix-Matrix Addition & Subtraction

Matrix-Matrix Addition and Subtraction is fairly easy and straightforward. The requirement is that the matrices have the same dimensions and the result is a Matrix that has also the same dimensions. You just add or subtract each value of the first Matrix with its corresponding value in the second Matrix.

2.2.8.3 Matrix Multiplication

Multiplying two Matrices together isn't that hard either if you know how to multiply a Matrix by a Vector. Note that you can only multiply Matrices together if the number of the first Matrix's columns matches the number of the second Matrix's rows. The result will be a Matrix with the same number of rows as the first Matrix and the same number of columns as the second Matrix. It works as follows:

You simply split the second Matrix into column-Vectors and multiply the first Matrix separately by each of these Vectors. Then you put the results in a new Matrix (without adding them up!).

2.2.8.3.1 Matrix Multiplication Properties

Matrix Multiplication has several properties that allow us to bundle a lot of computation into one Matrix multiplication. We will discuss them one by one below. We will start by explaining these concepts with Scalars and then with Matrices because this will give you a better understanding of the process.

1. Not Commutative

Scalar Multiplication is commutative but Matrix Multiplication is not. This means that when we are multiplying Scalars, 7*3 is the same as 3*7. But when we multiply Matrices by each other, A*B isn't the same as B*A.

2. Associative

Scalar and Matrix Multiplication are both associative. This means that the Scalar multiplication 3(5*3) is the same as (3*5)3 and that the Matrix multiplication A(B*C) is the same as (A*B)C.

3. **Distributive**

Scalar and Matrix Multiplication are also both distributive. This means that 3(5 + 3) is the same as 3*5 + 3*3 and that A(B+C) is the same as A*B + A*C.

4. **Identity Matrix**

The Identity Matrix is a special kind of Matrix but first, we need to define what an Identity is. The number 1 is an Identity because everything you multiply with 1 is equal to itself. Therefore, every Matrix that is multiplied by an Identity Matrix is equal to itself. For example, Matrix A times its Identity-Matrix is equal to A.

You can spot an Identity Matrix by the fact that it has ones along its diagonals and that every other value is zero. It is also a "squared matrix," meaning that its number of rows matches its number of columns. We previously discussed that Matrix multiplication is not commutative but there is one exception, namely if we multiply a

Matrix by an Identity Matrix. Therefore, the following equation is true: A*I = I*A = A

2.2.8.4 Inverse and Transpose

The Matrix inverse and the Matrix transpose are two special kinds of Matrix properties. Again, we will start by discussing how these properties relate to real numbers and then how they relate to Matrices.

2.2.9 Summary

In this section, you learned about the mathematical objects of Linear Algebra that are used in Machine Learning. You learned how to multiply, divide, add and subtract these mathematical objects. Furthermore, you have learned about the most important properties of Matrices and why they enable us to make more efficient computations. On top of that, you have learned what inverse and transpose Matrices are and what you can do with them. Although there are also other parts of Linear Algebra used in Machine Learning, this post gave you a proper introduction to the most important concepts.

2.3 Multivariate Calculus

Understanding calculus is central to understanding machine learning! You can think of calculus as simply a set of tools for analyzing the relationship between functions and their inputs. Typically, in machine learning, we are trying to find the inputs which enable a function to best match the data. We start this module from the basics, by recalling what a function is and where we might encounter one. Following this, we talk about the how, when sketching a function on a graph, the slope describes the rate of change off the output with respect to an input. Using this visual intuition, we next derive a robust mathematical definition of a derivative, which we then use to differentiate some interesting functions. Finally, by studying a few examples, we develop four handy time saving rules that enable us to speed up differentiation for many common scenarios.

Building on the foundations of the previous module, we now generalize our calculus tools to handle multivariable systems. This means we can take a function with multiple inputs and determine the influence of each of them separately. It would not be unusual for a machine learning method to require the analysis of a function with thousands of inputs, so we will also introduce the linear algebra structures necessary for storing the results of our multivariate calculus analysis in an orderly fashion.

2.3.1 Derivative

A derivative can be defined in two ways:

- Instantaneous rate of change (Physics)
- Slope of a line at a specific point (Geometry)

Both represent the same principle, but for our purposes it's easier to explain using the geometric definition.

$$\text{Slope} = \frac{Change\ in\ y}{Change\ in\ x}$$

A derivative output an expression we can use to calculate the instantaneous rate of change, or slope, at a single point on a line. After solving for the derivative, you can use it to calculate the slope at every other point on the line.

- Step by Step

Calculating the derivative is the same as calculating normal slope, however in this case we calculate the slope between our point and a point infinitesimally close to it. We use the variable h to represent this infinitesimally distance. Here are the steps:

1. Given the function:

$$f(x) = x^2$$

2. Increment x by a very small value $h(h=\Delta x)$
   f(x+h)=(x+h)²

3. Apply the slope formula

$$\frac{f(x+h) - f(x)}{h}$$

4. Simplify the equation

$$\frac{x^2 + 2xh + h^2 - x^2}{h}$$

$$\frac{2xh + h^2}{h} \quad \text{=2x+h}$$

5. Set h to 0 (the limit as h heads toward 0)

2x+0=2x

So, what does this mean? It means for the function f(x)=x2f(x)=x2, the slope at any point equals 2x2x. The formula is defined as:

$$\lim_{h\to 0} \frac{f(x+h) - f(x)}{h}$$

2.3.2 Machine Learning use Cases

Machine learning uses derivatives in optimization problems. Optimization algorithms like gradient descent use derivatives to decide whether to increase or decrease weights in order to maximize or minimize some objective (e.g. a model's accuracy or error functions). Derivatives also help us approximate nonlinear functions as linear functions (tangent lines), which have constant slopes. With a constant slope we can decide whether to move up or down the slope (increase or decrease our weights) to get closer to the target value (class label).

2.3.3 Chain Rule

The chain rule is a formula for calculating the derivatives of composite functions. Composite functions are functions composed of functions inside other function(s).

Given a composite function f(x)=A(B(x)), the derivative of f(x) equals the product of the derivative of A with respect to B(x) and the derivative of B with respect to x.

composite function derivative=outer function derivative × inner function derivative

For example,

$$f(x)=h(g(x))$$

The chain rule tells us the derivative of f(x) equals to

$$\frac{dy}{dx} = \frac{dh}{dg_\times}\frac{dg}{dx}$$

2.3.4 Gradient

A gradient is a vector that stores the partial derivatives of multivariable functions. It helps us calculate the slope at a specific point on a curve for functions with multiple independent variables. In order to calculate this more complex slope, we need to isolate each variable to determine how it impacts the output on its own. To do this we iterate through each of the variables and calculate the derivative of the function after holding all other variables constant. Each iteration produces a partial derivative which we store in the gradient.

2.3.5 Partial Derivative

In functions with 2 or more variables, the partial derivative is the derivative of one variable with respect to the others. If we change x, but hold all other variables constant, how does f (x, z) change? That's one partial derivative. The next variable is z. If we change z but hold xx constant, how does f (x, z) change? We store partial derivatives in a gradient, which represents the full derivative of the multivariable function.

2.4 Probability Theory

Why do we need probabilities when we already have such a great mathematical tooling? We have calculus to work with functions on the infinitesimal scale and to measure how they change. We developed algebra to solve equations, and we have dozens of other areas of mathematics that help us to tackle almost any kind of hard problem we can think of.

The difficult part is that we all live in a chaotic universe where things can't be measured exactly most of the time.

When we study real world processes we want to learn about numerous random events that distort our experiments. Uncertainty is everywhere and we must take it to be used for our needs. That is when probability theory and statistics come into play.

Nowadays those disciplines lie in the center of artificial intelligence, particle physics, social science, bio-informatics and in our everyday lives.

If we are getting to talk about statistics, it is better to settle on what is a probability. Actually, this question has no single best answer. We will go through various views on probability theory below.

2.4.1 Frequentist Probabilities

Imagine we were given a coin and want to check whether it is fair or not. How do we approach this? Let's try to conduct some experiments and record 1 if heads come up and 0 if we see tails. Repeat this 1000 tosses and count each 0 and 1. After we had some tedious time experimenting, we got those results: 600 heads (1s) and 400 tails (0s). If we then count how frequent heads or tails came up in the past, we will get 60% and 40% respectively. Those frequencies can be interpreted as probabilities of a coin coming up heads or tails. This is called a frequentist view on the probabilities.

2.4.2 Conditional Probabilities

Frequently we want to know the probability of an

event given some other event has occurred. We write conditional probability of an event A given event B as P (A | B).

2.4.3 Dependent and Independent Events

Events are called independent if the probability of one event does not influence the other in any way. Take for example the probability of rolling a dice and getting a 2 for the first time and for the second time. Those events are independent. We can state this as

$$P(\text{roll2}) = P(\text{roll2}_{\text{1st time}})P(\text{roll2}_{\text{2nd time}})$$

But why this formula works? First, let's rename events for 1st and 2nd tosses as A and B to remove notational clutter and then rewrite probability of a roll explicitly as joint probability of both rolls we had seen so far:

$$P(A,B) = P(A)P(B)$$

And now multiply and divide P(A) by P(B) (nothing changes, it can be cancelled out) and recall the definition of conditional probability:

$$P(A) = \frac{P(A)P(B)}{P(B)} = \frac{P(A,B)}{P(B)} = P(A|B)$$

If we read expression above from right to left we find that P(A | B) = P(A). Basically, this means that A is independent of B! The same argument goes for P(B) and we are done.

40

2.4.4 Distributions

What is a probability distribution anyways? It is a law that tells us probabilities of different possible outcomes in some experiment formulated as a mathematical function. As each function, a distribution may have some parameters to adjust its behavior.

When we measured relative frequencies of a coin toss event we have actually calculated a so-called empirical probability distribution. It turns out that many uncertain processes in our world can be formulated in terms of probability distributions. For example, our coin outcomes have a Bernoulli distribution and if we wanted to calculate a probability of heads after n trials we may use a Binomial distribution.

It is convenient to introduce a concept analogous to a variable that may be used in probabilistic environments—a random variable. Each random variable has some distribution assigned to it. Radom variables are written in upper case by convention, and we may use ~ symbol to specify a distribution assigned to a variable.

2.4.5 Basic Rules & Models

Probability gives the information about how likely an event can occur. Digging into the terminology of the probability:

Trial or Experiment: The act that leads to a result

41

with certain possibility.

Sample space: The set of all possible outcomes of an experiment.

Event: Non-empty subset of sample space is known as event.

So, in technical terms, probability is the measure of how likely an event is when an experiment is conducted.

Chapter 3: Programming Languages for Machine Learning

3.1 Programming Language

A programming language is a vocabulary and set of grammatical rules for instructing a computer or computing device to perform specific tasks. The term programming language usually refers to high-level languages, such as BASIC, C, C++, COBOL, Java, FORTRAN, Ada, and Pascal.

Each programming language has a unique set of keywords (words that it understands) and a special syntax for organizing program instructions.

High-level languages are designed to be easy to read and understand. This allows programmers to write source code in a natural fashion, using logical words and symbols. For example, reserved words like function, while, if, and else are used in most major programming languages. Symbols like <, >, ==, and != are common operators. Many high-level languages are similar enough that programmers can easily understand source code written in multiple languages.

Examples of high-level languages include C++, Java, Perl, and PHP. Languages like C++ and Java are called "compiled languages" since the source code must first be compiled in order to run. Languages like Perl and PHP are called "interpreted languages" since the source code can be run through an interpreter without being compiled. Generally, compiled languages are used to create software applications, while interpreted languages are used for running scripts, such as those used to generate content for dynamic websites.

3.2 Best Programming Languages for Machine Learning

There's so much more activity in machine learning than job offers in the West can describe, however, and peer opinions are of course very valuable but often conflicting and as such may confuse the novices. We turned instead to our hard data from 2,000+ data scientists and machine learning developers who responded to our latest survey about which languages they use and what projects they're working on—along with many other interesting things about their machine learning activities and training. Then, being data scientists ourselves, we couldn't help but run a few models to see which are the most important factors that are correlated to language selection. We compared the top-5 languages and the results prove that there is no simple answer to the "which language?" question. It depends on what you're trying to build, what your background is and why you got involved in machine learning in the first place.

3.2.1 Python

Python is considered to be in the first place in the list of all AI development languages due to the simplicity. The syntaxes belonging to python are very simple and can be easily learnt. Therefore, many AI algorithms can be easily implemented in it. Python takes short development time in comparison to other languages like Java, C++ or Ruby. Python supports object oriented, functional as well as procedure-oriented styles of programming. There are plenty of libraries in python, which make our tasks easier. For example: Numpy is a library for python that helps us to solve many scientific computations. Also, we have Pybrain, which is for using machine learning in Python.

3.2.2 R

R is one of the most effective language and environment for analyzing and manipulating the data for statistical purposes. Using R, we can easily produce well-designed publication-quality plot, including mathematical symbols and formulae where needed. Apart from being a general-purpose language, R has numerous of packages like RODBC, Gmodels, Class and Tm which are used in the field of machine learning. These packages make the implementation of machine learning algorithms easy, for cracking the business associated problems.

3.2.3 Lisp

Lisp is one of the oldest and the most suited languages for the development in AI. It was invented by John McCarthy, the father of Artificial Intelligence in 1958. It has the capability of processing the symbolic information effectively. It is also known for its excellent prototyping capabilities and easy dynamic creation of new objects, with automatic garbage collection. Its development cycle allows interactive evaluation of expressions and recompilation of functions or file while the program is still running. Over the years, due to advancement, many of these features have migrated into many other languages thereby affecting the uniqueness of Lisp.

3.2.4 Java

Java can also be considered as a good choice for AI development. Artificial intelligence has lot to do with search algorithms, artificial neural networks and genetic programming. Java provides many benefits: easy use, debugging ease, package services, simplified work with large-scale projects, graphical representation of data and better user interaction. It also has the incorporation of Swing and SWT (the Standard Widget Toolkit). These tools make graphics and interfaces look appealing and sophisticated.

3.2.5 Scala

Scala combines object-oriented and functional programming in one concise, high-level language. Scala's static types help avoid bugs in complex applications, and its JVM and JavaScript runtimes let you build high-performance systems with easy access to huge ecosystems of libraries. Scala is a modern multi-paradigm programming language designed to express common programming patterns in a concise, elegant, and type-safe way. Scala has been created by Martin Odersky and he released the first version in 2003. Scala smoothly integrates the features of object-oriented and functional languages. This tutorial explains the basics of Scala in a simple and reader-friendly way.

3.3 Tools for Machine Learning

Practical machine learning development has advanced at a remarkable pace. This is reflected by not only a rise in actual products based on, or offering, machine learning capabilities but also a rise in new development frameworks and methodologies, most of which are backed by open-source projects.

In fact, developers and researchers beginning a new project can be easily overwhelmed by the choice of frameworks offered out there. These new tools vary considerably — and striking a balance between keeping up with new trends and ensuring project stability and reliability can be hard.

The list below describes five of the most popular open-source machine learning frameworks, what they offer, and what use cases they can best be applied to.

3.3.1 TensorFlow

Made public and open-sourced two years ago, TensorFlow is Google's own internal framework for deep learning (artificial neural networks). It allows you to build any kind of neural network (and other computational models) by stacking the typical mathematical operations for NNs in a "computational graph."

The magic happens when the model is trained, and TensorFlow knows how to back-propagate errors through the computational graph, thus learning the correct parameters. TensorFlow is general enough to be used for building any type of network — from text to image classifiers, to more advanced models like generative adversarial neural networks (GANs), and even allows other frameworks to be built on top of it (see Keras and Edward down the list).

True, we could have selected other prominent deep learning frameworks that are equally as effective as TensorFlow-like Theano, Torch, or Caffe — but TensorFlow has risen in popularity so quickly that it's now arguably the de facto industry standard for deep learning (and yes, being developed and used by Google itself does lend it extra kudos.) It also has the most active and diverse ecosystem of developers and tools of all the DL frameworks.

3.3.2 Keras

Keras is a high-level interface for deep learning frameworks like Google's TensorFlow, Microsoft's CNTK, Amazon's MXNet, and more. Initially built from scratch by François Chollet in 2015, Keras quickly became the second-fastest growing deep learning framework after TensorFlow. This is easily explained by its declared purpose: to make drafting new DL models as easy as writing new methods in Python. This is why, for anyone who has struggled with building models using TensorFlow at all, Keras is nothing short of revolutionary-it allows you to easily create common types of neuron layers, select metrics, error function, and optimization method, and to train the model quickly and easily.

Its main power lies in its modularity: Almost every neural building block is available in the library (which is regularly updated with new ones), and they can all be easily composed on top of one another, to create more customized and elaborate models.

3.3.3 SciKit-Learn

With the recent explosion of deep learning, one may get the impression that other, more "classic" machine learning models are no longer in use. This is far from true — in fact, many common machine learning tasks can be solved using traditional models that were industry standard before the deep learning boom-and with much greater ease. While deep learning models are great at capturing patterns, it's often hard to explain what and how they have learned, an important requirement in many applications (see Lime, below, for model explanations). Plus, they're often very computationally expensive to train and deploy. Also, standard problems like clustering, dimensionality reduction, and feature selection can often be solved more easily using traditional models.

SciKit-learn is an academia-backed framework that has just celebrated its tenth anniversary. It contains almost every machine learning model imaginable — from linear and logistic regressors to SVM classifiers and random forests — and it has a huge toolbox of preprocessing methods like dimensionality reduction, text transformations, and many more.

3.3.4 Edward

Edward is one of the most promising and intriguing projects seen in the community in a while.

Created by Dustin Tran, a Ph.D. student at Columbia University and a researcher at Google, alongside a group of AI researchers and contributors, Edward is built on top of TensorFlow and fuses three fields: Bayesian statistics and machine learning, deep learning, and probabilistic programming.

It allows users to construct probabilistic graphical models (PGM). It can be used to build Bayesian neural networks, along with almost every model that can be represented as a graph and uses probabilistic representations. Its uses are still limited more to hardcore AI models than to real-world production, but since PGMs are proving increasingly useful in AI research, we can assume that practical uses will be found for these models in the near future.

Recently, Edward reached another impressive milestone, announcing that it will be officially integrated into the TensorFlow code base.

3.3.5 Lime

One of the biggest challenges with machine learning is explaining what your model has learned —in other words, debugging its internal representations. Say you've built a text classifier that works pretty well, but fails embarrassingly for some sentences. For example, you'd like to know which words in the sentence "Apple iPad Pro with red case" caused the model to classify the device as a surfboard instead of a tablet — finding out that the word "red" is more typical to surfboards than to smartphones, leading the model to a mistake. This can be done by inspecting the model's internal weights for each word in its vocabulary, a process that may become cumbersome for more complicated models with a lot of features and weights.

Lime is an easy-to-use Python package that does this for you in a more intelligent way. Taking a constructed model as input, it runs a second "meta" approximator of the learned model, which approximates the behavior of the model for different inputs. The output is an explainer for the model, identifying which parts of any input helped the model reach a decision and which didn't.

Chapter 4: Introduction to Python/R/Scala

4.1 Introduction to Python

Python is a widely used general-purpose, high level programming language. It was initially designed by Guido van Rossum in 1991 and developed by Python Software Foundation. It was mainly developed for emphasis on code readability, and its syntax allows programmers to express concepts in fewer lines of code.

Python is a programming language that lets you work quickly and integrate systems more efficiently.

There are two major Python versions- Python 2 and Python 3. Both are quite different.

4.1.1 Environment Setup

Before we start Python programming, we need to have an interpreter to interpret and run our programs.

Windows: There are many interpreters available freely to run Python scripts like IDLE (Integrated Development Environment) which is installed when you install the python software from http://python.org/

Linux: For Linux, Python comes bundled with the Linux.

4.1.2 Writing First Program

Following is first program in Python

```
# Script Begins
print("Hello World")
# Scripts Ends
```
Output: Hello World

54

4.2 Introduction to R

'R' is a programming language for data analysis and statistics. It is free, and very widely used by professional statisticians. It is also very popular in certain application areas, including bioinformatics. R is a dynamically typed interpreted language, and is typically used interactively. It has many built-in functions and libraries, and is extensible, allowing users to define their own functions and procedures using R, C or Fortran. It also has a simple object system.

4.2.1 Environment Setup

Windows: You can download the Windows installer version of R from R-3.2.2 for Windows (32/64 bit) and save it in a local directory.

As it is a Windows installer (.exe) with a name "R-version-win.exe". You can just double click and run the installer accepting the default settings. If your Windows is 32-bit version, it installs the 32-bit version. But if your windows is 64-bit, then it installs both the 32-bit and 64-bit versions.

After installation you can locate the icon to run the Program in a directory structure "R\R3.2.2\bin\i386\Rgui.exe" under the Windows Program Files. Clicking this icon brings up the R-GUI which is the R console to do R Programming.

Linux: R is available as a binary for many versions of Linux at the location R Binaries.

The instruction to install Linux varies from flavor to flavor. These steps are mentioned under each type of Linux version in the mentioned link. However, if you are in a hurry, then you can use yum command to install R as follows –

```
$ yum install R
```

Above command will install core functionality of R programming along with standard packages, still you need additional package, then you can launch R prompt as follows –

```
$ R

R version 3.2.0 (2015-04-16) -- "Full of Ingredients"

Copyright (C) 2015 The R Foundation for Statistical Computing

Platform: x86_64-redhat-linux-gnu (64-bit)


R is free software and comes with ABSOLUTELY NO WARRANTY.

You are welcome to redistribute it under certain conditions.

Type 'license()' or 'licence()' for distribution details.

R is a collaborative project with many contributors.

Type 'contributors()' for more information and
```

'citation()' on how to cite R or R packages in publications.

Type 'demo()' for some demos, 'help()' for on-line help, or

'help.start()' for an HTML browser interface to help.

Type 'q()' to quit R.

>

4.2.2 Writing First Program

Once you have R environment setup, then it's easy to start your R command prompt by just typing the following command at your command prompt −

$ R

This will launch R interpreter and you will get a prompt > where you can start typing your program as follows −

> myString <- "Hello, World!"

> print (myString)

[1] "Hello, World!"

4.3 Scala

Scala is a modern multi-paradigm programming language designed to express common programming patterns in a concise, elegant, and type-safe way. Scala has been created by Martin Odersky and he released the first version in 2003. Scala smoothly integrates the features of object-oriented and functional languages. This tutorial explains the basics of Scala in a simple and reader-friendly way.

Scala, short for Scalable Language, is a hybrid functional programming language. It was created by Martin Odersky. Scala smoothly integrates the features of object-oriented and functional languages. Scala is compiled to run on the Java Virtual Machine. Many existing companies, who depend on Java for business-critical applications, are turning to Scala to boost their development productivity, applications scalability and overall reliability.

4.3.1 Environment Setup

Scala can be installed on any UNIX flavored or Windows based system. Before you start installing Scala on your machine, you must have Java 1.8 or greater installed on your computer.

Follow the steps given below to install Scala.

Step 1: Verify your Java Installation:

First of all, you need to have Java Software Development Kit (SDK) installed on your system. To verify this, execute any of the following two

58

commands depending on the platform you are working on.

If the Java installation has been done properly, then it will display the current version and specification of your Java installation.

Windows:
Open Command Console

and type −\>java −version

Linux:

Open Command terminal and type −

$java −version

We assume that the readers of this tutorial have Java SDK version 1.8.0_31 installed on their system.

In case you do not have Java SDK, download its current version from http://www.oracle.com/technetwork/java/ja vase/downloads/index.html and install it.

Setup 2: Set your Java Environment

Windows: Set JAVA_HOME to C:\ProgramFiles\java\jdk1.7.0_60

Linux: Export JAVA_HOME=/usr/local/java-current

Append the full path of Java compiler location to the System Path

Windows: Append the String "C:\Program Files\Java\jdk1.7.0_60\bin" to the end of the system variable PATH.

Linux: Export PATH=$PATH:$JAVA_HOME/bin/

Execute the command java -version from the command prompt as explained above.

Setup 3: Install Scala

You can download Scala from http://www.scala-lang.org/downloads. At the time of writing this tutorial, I downloaded 'scala-2.11.5-installer.jar'. Make sure you have admin privilege to proceed. Now, execute the following command at the command prompt –

Windows:

\>java –jar scala-2.11.5-installer.jar\>

Linux:

$java –jar scala-2.9.0.1-installer.jar

Finally, open a new command prompt and type Scala -version and press Enter. You should see the following –

Windows:

\>scala -version

Linux:

$scala -version

4.3.2 Writing First Program

Open the command prompt and use the following command to open Scala.

\>scala

If Scala is installed in your system, the following output will be displayed –

Welcome to Scala version 2.9.0.1

Type in expressions to have them evaluated.

Type :help for more information.

Type the following text to the right of the Scala prompt and press the Enter key –

scala> println("Hello, Scala!");

It will produce the following result –

Hello, Scala!

Chapter 5: Introduction to MLlib
(Apache Spark)

5.1 Introduction

Apache Spark is a lightning-fast cluster computing designed for fast computation. It was built on top of Hadoop MapReduce and it extends the MapReduce model to efficiently use more types of computations which includes Interactive Queries and Stream Processing. This is a brief tutorial that explains the basics of Spark Core programming.

The main feature of Spark is its in-memory cluster computing that increases the processing speed of an application.

Spark is designed to cover a wide range of workloads such as batch applications, iterative algorithms, interactive queries and streaming. Apart from supporting all these workloads in a respective system, it reduces the management burden of maintaining separate tools.

5.1.1 Features of Apache Spark

Apache Spark has following features.

- Speed – Spark helps to run an application in Hadoop cluster, up to 100 times faster in memory, and 10 times faster when running on disk. This is possible by reducing number of read/write operations to disk. It stores the intermediate processing data in memory.
- Supports multiple languages – Spark

64

provides built-in APIs in Java, Scala, or Python. Therefore, you can write applications in different languages. Spark comes up with 80 high-level operators for interactive querying.

- Advanced Analytics – Spark not only supports 'Map' and 'reduce'. It also supports SQL queries, Streaming data, Machine learning (ML), and Graph algorithms.

5.2 MLlib

Spark provides a machine learning library known as MLlib. Spark MLlib provides various machine learning algorithms such as classification, regression, clustering, and collaborative filtering. It also provides tools such as featurization, pipelines, persistence, and utilities for handling linear algebra operations, statistics and data handling.

5.2.1 Overview

Spark MLlib is used to perform machine learning in Apache Spark. MLlib consists popular algorithms and utilities.

MLlib Overview:

- spark.mllib contains the original API built on top of RDDs. It is currently in maintenance mode.
- spark.ml provides higher level API built on top of Data Frames for constructing ML pipelines. spark.ml is the primary Machine Learning API for Spark at the moment.

5.2.2 Spark MLlib Tools

Spark MLlib provides the following tools:

- ML Algorithms: ML Algorithms form the core of MLlib. These include common learning algorithms such as classification, regression, clustering and collaborative filtering.

66

- Featurization: Featurization includes feature extraction, transformation, dimensionality reduction and selection.
- Pipelines: Pipelines provide tools for constructing, evaluating and tuning ML Pipelines.
- Persistence: Persistence helps in saving and loading algorithms, models and Pipelines.
- Utilities: Utilities for linear algebra, statistics and data handling.

5.2.3   MLlib Algorithms

The popular algorithms and utilities in Spark MLlib are:

- Basic Statistics
- Regression
- Classification
- Recommendation System
- Clustering
- Dimensionality Reduction
- Feature Extraction
- Optimization

5.2.3.1 Basic Statistics

Basic Statistics includes the most basic of machine learning techniques. These include:

- Summary Statistics: Examples include mean, variance, count, max, min and numNonZeros.
- Correlations: Spearman and Pearson are some ways to find correlation.
- Stratified Sampling: These include sampleBykey and sampleByKeyExact.
- Hypothesis Testing: Pearson's chi-squared test is an example of hypothesis testing.
- Random Data Generation: RandomRDDs, Normal and Poisson are used to generate random data

5.2.3.2 Regression

Regression analysis is a statistical process for estimating the relationships among variables. It includes many techniques for modeling and analyzing several variables when the focus is on the relationship between a dependent variable and one or more independent variables. More specifically, regression analysis helps one understand how the typical value of the dependent variable changes when any one of the independent variables is varied, while the other independent variables are held fixed.

Regression analysis is widely used for prediction and forecasting, where its use has substantial overlap with the field of machine learning. Regression analysis is also used to understand which among the independent variables are related to the dependent variable, and to explore the forms of these relationships. In restricted circumstances, regression analysis can be used to infer causal relationships between the independent and dependent variables.

5.2.3.3 Classification

Classification is the problem of identifying to which of a set of categories (sub-populations) a new observation belongs, on the basis of a training set of data containing observations (or instances) whose category membership is known. It is an example of pattern recognition.

Here, an example would be assigning a given email into "spam" or "non-spam" classes or assigning a diagnosis to a given patient as described by observed characteristics of the patient (gender, blood pressure, presence or absence of certain symptoms, etc.).

5.2.3.4 Recommendation System

A recommendation system is a subclass of information filtering system that seeks to predict the "rating" or "preference" that a user would give to an item. Recommender systems have become increasingly popular in recent years, and are utilized in a variety of areas including movies, music, news, books, research articles, search queries, social tags, and products in general.

Recommender systems typically produce a list of recommendations in one of two ways – through collaborative and content-based filtering or the personality-based approach.

Collaborative Filtering approaches building a model from a user's past behavior (items previously purchased or selected and/or numerical ratings given to those items) as well as similar decisions made by other users. This model is then used to predict items (or ratings for items) that the user may have an interest in.

Content-Based Filtering approaches utilize a series of discrete characteristics of an item in order to recommend additional items with similar properties.

5.2.3.5 Clustering

Clustering is the task of grouping a set of objects in such a way that objects in the same group (called a cluster) are more similar (in some sense or another) to each other than to those in other groups (clusters). So, it is the main task of exploratory data mining, and a common technique for statistical data analysis, used in many fields, including machine learning, pattern recognition, image analysis, information retrieval, bioinformatics, data compression and computer graphics.

5.2.3.6 Feature Extraction

Feature Extraction starts from an initial set of measured data and builds derived values (features) intended to be informative and non-redundant, facilitating the subsequent learning and generalization steps, and in some cases leading to better human interpretations. This is related to dimensionality reduction.

5.2.3.7 Optimization

Optimization is the selection of the best element (with regard to some criterion) from some set of available alternatives.

In the simplest case, an optimization problem consists of maximizing or minimizing a real function by systematically choosing input values from within an allowed set and computing the value of the function. The generalization of optimization theory and techniques to other formulations comprises a large area of applied mathematics. More generally, optimization includes finding "best available" values of some objective function given a defined domain (or input), including a variety of different types of objective functions and different types of domains.

5.2.3.8 Dimensionality Reduction

Dimensionality Reduction is the process of reducing the number of random variables under consideration, via obtaining a set of principal variables. It can be divided into feature selection and feature extraction.

Feature Selection: Feature selection finds a subset of the original variables (also called features or attributes).

Feature Extraction: This transforms the data in the high-dimensional space to a space of fewer dimensions. The data transformation may be linear, as in Principal Component Analysis (PCA), but many nonlinear dimensionality reduction techniques also exist.

Chapter 6: Overview of Available ML Libraries

6.1 Libraries of Python

There are tons of machine learning libraries already written for Python. You can choose one of the hundreds of libraries based on your use-case, skill, and need for customization.

6.1.1 TensorFlow

This is the newest neural network library on the list. Just having been released in the past few days, TensorFlow is a high-level neural network library that helps you program your network architectures while avoiding the low-level details. The focus is more on allowing you to express your computation as a data flow graph, which is much more suited to solving complex problems.

It is mostly written in C++, which includes the Python bindings, so you don't have to worry about sacrificing performance. One of my favorite features is the flexible architecture, which allows you to deploy it to one or more CPUs or GPUs in a desktop, server, or mobile device all with the same API. Not many, if any, libraries can make that claim.

It was developed for the Google Brain project and is now used by hundreds of engineers throughout the company, so there's no question whether it's capable of creating interesting solutions.

6.1.2 Scikit-learn

The scikit-learn library is definitely one of, if not the most, popular ML libraries out there among all languages (at the time of this writing). It has a huge number of features for data mining and data analysis, making it a top choice for researches and developers alike.

Its built-on top of the popular NumPy, SciPy, and matplotlib libraries, so it'll have a familiar feel to it for the many people that already use these libraries. Although, compared to many of the other libraries listed below, this one is a bit lower level and tends to act as the foundation for many other ML implementations.

6.1.3 Theano

Theano is a machine learning library that allows you to define, optimize, and evaluate mathematical expressions involving multi-dimensional arrays, which can be a point of frustration for some developers in other libraries. Like scikit-learn, Theano also tightly integrates with NumPy. The transparent use of the GPU makes Theano fast and painless to set up, which is pretty crucial for those just starting out. Although some have described it as more of a research tool than production use, so use it accordingly.

6.1.4 Pylearn2

Pylearn2 differs from scikit-learn in that Pylearn2

aims to provide great flexibility and make it possible for a researcher to do almost anything, while scikit-learn aims to work as a "black box" that can produce good results even if the user does not understand the implementation.

Keep in mind that Pylearn2 may sometimes wrap other libraries such as scikit-learn when it makes sense to do so, so you're not getting 100% custom-written code here. This is great, however, since most of the bugs have already been worked out.

6.1.5 Pyevolve

One of the more exciting and different areas of neural network research is in the space of genetic algorithms. A genetic algorithm is basically just a search heuristic that mimics the process of natural selection. It essentially tests a neural network on some data and gets feedback on the network's performance from a fitness function. Then it iteratively makes small, random changes to the network and proceeds to test it again using the same data. Networks with higher fitness scores win out and are then used as the parent to new generations.

Pyevolve provides a great framework to build and execute this kind of algorithm. Although the author has stated that as of v0.6 the framework is also supporting genetic programming, so in the near future the framework will lean more towards being an Evolutionary Computation framework than a just simple GA framework.

6.1.6 NuPIC

NuPIC is another library that provides to you some different functionality than just your standard ML algorithms. It is based on a theory of the neocortex called Hierarchical Temporal Memory (HTM). HTMs can be viewed as a type of neural network, but some of the theory is a bit different.

Fundamentally, HTMs are a hierarchical, time-based memory system that can be trained on various data. It is meant to be a new computational framework that mimics how memory and computation are intertwined within our brains.

6.1.7 Numpy

Numpy is considered as one of the most popular machine learning library in Python. TensorFlow and other libraries uses Numpy internally for performing multiple operations on Tensors. Array interface is the best and the most important feature of Numpy.

This interface can be utilized for expressing images, sound waves, and other binary raw streams as an array of real numbers in N-dimensional. For implementing this library for machine learning having knowledge of Numpy is important for developers.

6.1.8 Eli5

Most often the results of machine learning model predictions are not accurate, and Eli5 machine learning library built in Python helps in overcoming this challenge. It is a combination of visualization and debug all the machine learning models and track all working steps of an algorithm.

Moreover, Eli5 supports wother libraries XGBoost, lightning, scikit-learn, and sklearn-crfsuite libraries. All the above-mentioned libraries can be used to perform different tasks using each one of them.

6.1.9 PyTorch

PyTorch is the largest machine learning library that allow developers to perform tensor computations with acceleration of GPU, creates dynamic computational graphs, and calculate gradients automatically. Other than this, PyTorch offers rich APIs for solving application issues related to neural networks.

This machine learning library is based on Torch, which is an open source machine library implemented in C with a wrapper in Lua. This machine library in Python was introduced in 2017, and since its inception, the library is gaining popularity and attracting increasing number of machine learning developers.

6.1.10 Pandas

Pandas is a machine learning library in Python that provides data structures of high-level and a wide variety of tools for analysis. One of the great feature of this library is the ability to translate complex operations with data using one or two commands. Pandas have so many inbuilt methods for grouping, combining data, and filtering, as well as time-series functionality.

All these are followed by outstanding speed indicators.

Currently, there are fewer releases of Pandas library which includes hundreds of new features, bug fixes, enhancements, and changes in API. The improvements in pandas regards its ability to group and sort data, select best suited output for the apply method, and provides support for performing custom types operations.

6.1.11 Pattern

This is more of a 'full suite' library as it provides not only some ML algorithms but also tools to help you collect and analyze data. The data mining portion helps you collect data from web services like Google, Twitter, and Wikipedia. It also has a web crawler and HTML DOM parser. The nice thing about including these tools is how easy it makes it to both collect and train on data in the same program.

79

6.1.12 Caffe

Caffe is a library for machine learning in vision applications. You might use it to create deep neural networks that recognize objects in images or even to recognize a visual style.

Seamless integration with GPU training is offered, which is highly recommended for when you're training on images. Although this library seems to be mostly for academics and research, it should have plenty of uses for training models for production use as well.

Chapter 7: Conclusion

7.1 Conclusion

Over the past two decades Machine Learning has become one of the mainstays of information technology and with that, a rather central, albeit usually hidden, part of our life. With the ever-increasing amounts of data becoming available there is good reason to believe that smart data analysis will become even more pervasive as a necessary ingredient for technological progress.

We hope you have enjoyed learning about "Guide for Beginners with R/Python/Scala". Everyone knows about AI. Usually, when we hear that term, we picture robots that can perform human tasks better than we can. However, we're still a very long way from building robots that will replace us; many of the activities you do every day are surprisingly complex. So, while much of the potential of AI still remains unrealized, machine learning is very real and already here.

Machine learning (ML) has recently gained in popularity, spurred by well-publicized advances like deep learning and widespread commercial interest in big data analytics. Despite the enthusiasm, some renowned experts of the field have expressed skepticism, which is justifiable given the disappointment with the previous wave of neural networks and other AI techniques.

Machine learning can be considered a part of AI, as most of what we imagine when we think about AI is machine-learning based. Machine learning is, at its core, the process of granting a machine or model access to data and letting it learn for itself. The best way to understand the potential of machine learning is to explore how people and companies are currently taking advantage of it.